BRITAIN
An Aerial Close-up

CLB 1044
© 1988 Illustrations and text: Colour Library Books Ltd, Godalming, Surrey, England.
Display and text filmsetting by Acesetters Ltd, Richmond, Surrey, England.
Printed and bound in Barcelona, Spain, by Cronion, S.A.
All rights reserved.
ISBN 0 86283 270 5

BRITAIN
An Aerial Close~up

Written and Designed by
PHILIP CLUCAS

Produced by
David Gibbon

COOMBE BOOKS

70 Holyhead
60 Conway
67 South Stack
61 Rhuddlan Castle
71 The Menai Suspension Bridge
69 Portmeirion
64 The Snowdon Horseshoe
65 Tryfan
62 Harlech Castle
66 Solva
68 Milford Haven
63 Pembroke

84 Buxton
85 Ladybower Reservoir
83 Lincoln
77 Holkham Hall
82 Boston
76 Castle Rising
75 King's Lynn
79 The Fens
74 Norwich

57 Birmingham
56 Rugby
59 Warwick
58 Stratford-upon-Avon
55 The Malvern Hills
30 Chipping Campden
53 Tewkesbury
32 Blenheim Palace
52 Bourton-on-the-Water
28 and 29 The City of Oxford
33 Mapledurham House
35 Marlborough

78 Ely
81 Cambridge
80 King's College
73 Finchingfield
72 Harwich

20 and 21 Westminster
16 and 19 The City
18 St Paul's
22 and 23 Chelsea
24 Hampton Court
17 The Tower
2 Ramsgate
3 Canterbury
15 Reigate
6 Knole
12 Leeds Castle
14 Polesden Lacey
7 Hever
9 Sissinghurst Castle
5 Penshurst
8 Scotney Castle
4 Cranbrook
13 Bodiam Castle
10 Rye
11 The Storrington Downs

1 The Severn Estuary
50 and 51 Bath
48 Wells
37 Stonehenge
38 Wilton House
36 Longford Castle
39 Stourhead
34 Salisbury
26 Lyndhurst
49 Montacute House
27 Brockenhurst
25 Beaulieu Abbey

41 Pendeen Watch
40 St Ives
44 Talland Bay
45 Longships Lighthouse
42 St Michael's Mount
43 Coverack
47 Cadgwith

*The South and West of England,
East Anglia and Wales*

Introduction: The Landscape Below

The natural landscape of the British Isles is astonishingly rich and varied, and the trace of man upon that landscape – in his monuments and in his architecture – is infinitely diverse and splendid. Thus are forged the two features, of nature and of heritage, that make Britain unique among the countries of the world. The past is enshrined in the landscape, and the changes that the British (an amalgam of ancient races – of Celt, Roman, Jute, Angle, Saxon, Norse and Norman) have made upon it. Millennia of geological force and climatic upheaval have shaped the countryside, and centuries of commercial and social interplay have conspired to weave an historical tapestry of great intricacy and colour which is ever present and always awaiting discovery.

Over the length and breadth of Britain there could be no finer way of discovering the land's scenic beauty and appreciating the jewels that mankind has placed therein – be it ancient earthwork, medieval cathedral, bare Gothic abbey or the ruined husks of castles – than to see them from the air. A bird's-eye view offers a vast panorama, at once lyrical and documentary, and much that is too vast to comprehend from the ground can be placed within an all-embracing perspective and seen anew.

The present volume reflects the striking diversity to be found within Britain, and of the 120 specially commissioned photographs included in this, one of the largest and most lavishly illustrated aerial surveys of Britain ever published, each has been selected for the insight that it affords into the natural wonders and architectural glories of these Isles. In the succeeding colour plates and accompanying text the progression through aerial Britain is charted; encompassing all the regions of this enchanted land and, because the undertaking occupied a whole year's duration, the landscape below is to be seen in all the vibrant and varied shades of the seasons.

The journey starts in the South-East, whose tranquil beauties of rolling chalk downland are epitomised by the view of the Storrington Hills *(plate 11)* – enfolded within a cowl of snow, yet dappled with innumerable shades of blue. The area was the invasion coast of old, and along her hilltop trackways came wave after wave of Neolithic farmers and Bronze Age warriors. At a later age, lowland paths rang with the cries of the Legions and, supplanting Rome, came Saxon, Jutish and Anglian families to turn the great wooded valleys of the Weald into fertile expanses of plough and pasture land. The legacies of these ancestral races are to be found in the Chichester and Canterbury *(plate 3)* Roman street plans: the latter's cathedral, under St Augustine and Saxon patronage, developed into the Mother Church of the English nation. The last successful invasion was that of Duke William of Normandy, whose gaunt bastions speak volumes about the iron rule of the Norman dynasty. From the 13th to the 15th century the old 'Invasion Coastline' bristled with ragstone castles of England's new 'Defensive Shore'. They number among their finest Bodiam *(plate 13)* and Leeds Castle *(plate 12)* – and of the numerous fortified towns walled against the French, the Cinque port of Rye *(plate 10)* in Sussex is one of the most complete. Today, the centuries have cast their spell over them, and they are tinged the colour of honey by time-encrusted lichens – softened at places such as Hever *(plate 7)* and Scotney *(plate 8)* by intimate and 'romantic' gardens, and at Sissinghurst by Tudor knot gardens and wild roses that seemingly ramble at will over the warm red brick of the castle's towering gatehouse *(plate 9)*.

From the counties of Kent, Sussex and Surrey, the progression is to Dunbar's *'Flower of Cities all'* – London – founded through Roman imperialism and massively fortified by the Conqueror's great sentinel of the White Tower at the Tower of London *(plate 17)*; which incorporates bull's blood in its mortar to stand for eternity.

The square mile of the Romano-British capital has developed into the wealthiest square mile on Earth – the City *(plates 16 and 19)*. In the Middle Ages the City was the home of merchants, and the City of Westminster *(plate 21)* the home of kings. The latter had their abbey church dedicated to St Peter, and the former a cathedral dedicated to St Paul. The cathedral was destroyed in the fire of 1666, and raised again *(plate 18)* under the guiding genius of Sir Christopher Wren.

From London the way leads westwards, over Wolsey's Thames-side palace at Hampton Court *(plate 24)*, and upstream along the great river as it passes quiet country towns like Henley *(plate 31)* and snug, unhurried villages whose beech-laden hills fall precipitously to the water meads below. From here the Thames cuts its meandering course through the chalk-lands of Southern England to the precious architectural gem of Oxford *(plates 28 and 29)*. This line of the Thames was, in ancient times, the northern boundary of Wessex, whence England as a nation was wrested from the grip of Dane. Here, in Hampshire and Wiltshire, are the heartlands of the Kingdom of Alfred, to whom history awards the simple but supreme accolade, *'the Great'*. It was he who built England's first navy – enabling the modern port of Southampton to trace its origins back to the days of the *Anglo-Saxon Chronicle* – and fostering that proud affinity with the sea which filled the ledgers at places such as Buckler's Hard with orders for merchantmen bound for the Eastern Seas and men o'war for the Navy's Deep Water Fleet.

The Wessex landscape of today is one of bright harvest sunshine, where summer is shrouded in the rich blue of that *'unattainable flower of the sky'*; and the winter scene is one of clouds racing across the countryside, with here and there a gleam of sunlight to flame a blackened hedgerow amber for a few seconds and then to pass onward to where the sun picks out the tower of a church in silver, or the gabled end of a brick-built cottage in military scarlet. Light and shadow everywhere change and exchange upon the chalk scarp of the hills, the evanescent sunshine clarifying small fields without number, whilst into the peace steals the sound of church bells; from the lofty heights of Salisbury's peerless spire *(plate 34)* and from Sherborne's abbey; the distant downland hamlets and from New Forest villages such as those at leafy Brockenhurst *(plate 27)* and Lyndhurst *(plate 26)*.

This realm of Alfred – where blood was shed for his dream of England – was ancient long before the Saxons settled here. At least three thousand years earlier, a very different breed of men had grazed their sheep on the hills and tilled the southern fields. Their monuments abound in the countryside still – sarsens, dolmens and megaliths stand in meadow and on bare downs, like human figures frozen for all time, marking the mysterious route to Wiltshire's Neolithic cathedral. More than any other place, Stonehenge *(plate 37)* evokes the darkest and most distant reaches of history.

From the centre of a religion long-lost to the knowledge of man, the western lands of Devon, Cornwall and Somerset – the next visited in this aerial route through Britain – hold a tradition that stretches back to the childhood of Christ Himself. William Blake, when he asked:

> *And did those feet in ancient time,*
> *Walk upon England's mountains green?*
> *And was the Holy Lamb of God*
> *On England's pleasant pastures seen?*
> *And did the Countenance Divine*
> *Shine forth upon our clouded hills?*

was referring to the green landscape of the West. Here also, according to lore, journeyed Joseph of Arimathea, bringing with him the Chalice of the Last Supper – the Holy Grail. It should not be forgotten that the first Christian Church in Britain was never totally destroyed by the heathen invaders, and such soaring monuments as Wells Cathedral *(plate 48)* can trace with pride a continuance of worship that stretches back to an early Celtic fane.

It is pleasant to think of the West Country, with its long coastline abutting the surging swell of two seas and the crashing breakers of the open ocean – seen in all its savage splendour at Land's End *(plate 41)* – as though it were a country in itself. Indeed, there is a sense in which it has always been so, for since man first roamed these Isles the Somerset Levels, with their all but impenetrable landscape of marsh and lagoon, have formed a barrier between the lands of Devon and Cornwall and the rest of England. Early lines of communication consisted of tortuous trackways which always followed the highest contour to avoid the steep fall of streams and the area's tidal estuaries. The trails through Somerset and Dorset, where they were low-lying or progressed through forest, were virtually impassable; in some parts of these counties this remained true right up to the advent of the railways. Thus was born the West Countryman's close affinity with the wild-waters of his native coastline (sea-voyage was less fraught with hazard than overland travel), forging that proud kinship with the sea forever evocative of Elizabeth's reign, when it held the destiny of the English Realm. There are scores of tiny fishing villages such as Coverack *(plate 43)* and Cadgwith *(plate 47)* which nestle beside harsh granite cliffs overlooking the broad surges of the bar and the everlasting thunder of the long Atlantic swell.

The Bristol Channel *(plate 1)* leads the way northeastwards – past the greatest of ancient ports, Bristol, whose graceful neighbour Bath *(plates 50 and 51)* has been acclaimed the most elegant of all British cities – to delve into the rolling landscape of the Severn and Avon Valleys. Here are found elm-fringed meadows, and orchards laden with damson, cherry, apple and pear. It is the verdant heartland of England *(plate 58)*, so beloved of Shakespeare; the misty-green vale from which Elgar drew his music and, centuries beforehand, Langland his vision of *'Piers Plowman'*. The land is naturally at its most beautiful at Eastertide, when its orchards are enveloped in a white foam of blossom. In pockets of wayside vegetation bluebells are found in such profusion that coppice-margins and hedgebanks are *'washed wet like lakes'* bathed in pools of light – whose sheen continually changes as the drooping flower heads swirl in heavily-scented breezes. Above the beauties of the Severn rises the medieval Abbey of Tewkesbury *(plate 53)*; its construction meticulously honed to complement the countryside's unique qualities of light – an effect best observed (in the words of Langland's poetry), *'In a somer seson whan soft was the sonne'*. Indeed, it is this element of luminosity – of gathering light – that best characterises the jagged Malvern Hills *(plate 55)* to the west, and illuminates the gentle, bow-headed landscape of the Cotswolds which stretch beyond the vale to south and to east. It is here, in towns such as Bourton-on-the-

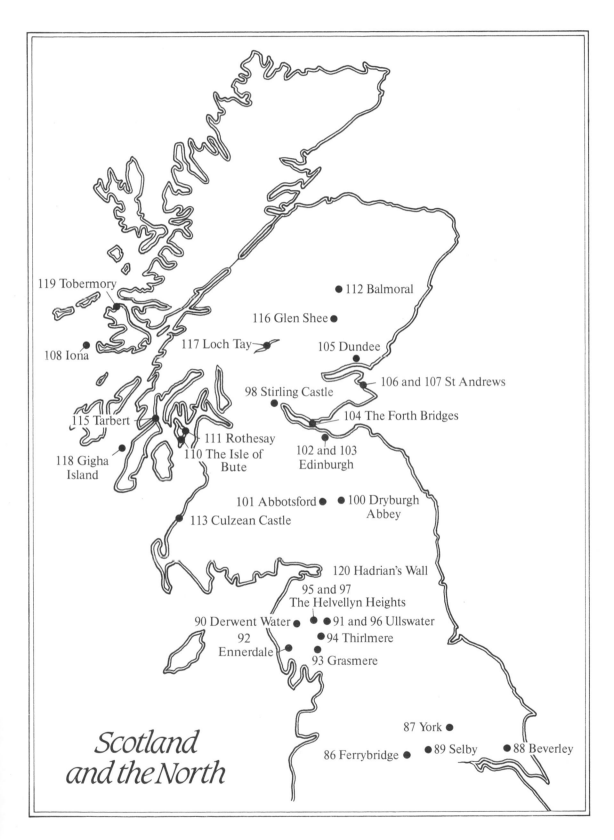

119 Tobermory

112 Balmoral

116 Glen Shee

117 Loch Tay

108 Iona

105 Dundee

106 and 107 St Andrews

98 Stirling Castle

104 The Forth Bridges

115 Tarbert

111 Rothesay

110 The Isle of
Bute

102 and 103
Edinburgh

118 Gigha
Island

101 Abbotsford

100 Dryburgh
Abbey

113 Culzean Castle

120 Hadrian's Wall

95 and 97
The Helvellyn Heights

90 Derwent Water

91 and 96 Ullswater

92
Ennerdale

94 Thirlmere

93 Grasmere

87 York

86 Ferrybridge

89 Selby

88 Beverley

*Scotland
and the North*

Water *(plate 52)* and Chipping Campden *(plate 30)* with their predominance of honey-brown masonry, that the stones themselves appear to glow.

Travelling westwards once again, the exhilarating vistas of Wales are encountered in the ancient southern Principality of Deheubarth, where a chain of English Marcher castles stretch from the Forest of Dean to Dyfed's Atlantic headland. They number, among their finest, Caerphilly Castle, Carew, Chepstow and Pembroke *(plate 63)*, whose towns grew up beneath their Norman walls; quiet places nowadays that seem to belong to their past, half asleep in the shadow of their castle crags. Thus, through great medieval upheavals – the crumbling power of the Llewellyn princes; the encroachment of Marcher fiefs; the campaigns in northern Wales of the Plantagenet kings, who built fortresses at Conway *(plate 60)*, Rhuddlan *(plate 61)* and Harlech *(plate 62)*; and the culminating tragedy of Owain Glyndwr – has the flower of Celtic independence retreated; seemingly into the mountainous fastness of the surrounding countryside.

Wales is an extraordinary mixture of the obvious and the recondite, a country of romantic legends and shattered bastions. Yet the overpowering spirit of the landscape is one of Gothic drama – a wild, mountainous terrain of vast, indigo, cloud-misted distances, pervaded by the sound of sweet-water and birdsong. Here is a depth of vision leading into the centre of an almost untouchable world of clear light, moorland and lovely valleys. However, soaring above all, dominating all, are the mountains – of the Cambrian Range, of Tryfan *(plate 65)*, and of a host of others – yet it is to the ethereal, azure mass of Snowdon *(plate 64)* that the focus of bardic song and sentiment has turned throughout the ages.

From the ancient savagery and power of the West's moors, mountains and seascapes, we next cross the country to the relatively flat lands of East Anglia – where the landscape is typically one of sweeping views in low relief. It comprises areas of Fenlands, whose dark waters cowl sedge-swamps and reed-beds in shadowed morasses; of estuary; mile upon mile of mud flats, and 'meals' – vast sand dunes – a lonely kingdom of wildfowl, where wading birds and geese flock in their thousands. However, in direct contrast to these desolate spots where nature is racked by piercing winds driven inland from the North Sea, the majority of the eastern counties is given over to intensive arable farming – such as that which surrounds the village of Finchingfield *(plate 73)* in Essex – whose rich, dark soils are numbered among the most fertile in the world. Here the landscape is entirely pastoral, swelling into gentle, golden ridges, the crests of which carry hedgerows, occasional coppice woodland and, in the vales, stream-splashed water meads and farmsteads which, in the Middle Ages, supplied the wool that gave rise to the trading ports of Boston *(plate 82)* and King's Lynn *(plate 75)*; and supplied the wealth that prospered the great cathedral cities of Lincoln *(plate 83)*, Norwich *(plate 74)* and Ely *(plate 78)*, whose

Norman towers and peerless octagon stand out defiantly against the violent light of the endless flats of the Great Level – representing the finest flower of medieval architecture.

From the Fenland of the Wash, and the Wolds of Lincolnshire, the journey is northwards to the ancient Saxon Kingdom of Northumbria and the wild, often windswept counties which share a history as turbulent as any in Britain. Castles such as those of Warkworth and Bamburgh are eloquent testimony to the bloodshed and conflict of the past; yet it is the Roman Wall *(plate 120)* which, more than anything else, speaks of its own rueful strength of purpose.

In the days before industrialisation laid wide-grasping hands upon the valleys and rivers, there was scarcely a square mile of land lying between the waters of the Humber and the Tweed which had not some charm and beauty to reveal. But when the demand for iron-ore and coal increased – the latter now feeding power stations such as Ferrybridge *(plate 86)* – stretches of hitherto solitary land became utterly changed in aspect and character. Fortunately the major part of the northern landscape remains unscarred and still forms one of the largest tracts of unspoilt countryside in England. The Peak country of Derbyshire coninues to be an expanse of loveliness – especially around the spa town of Buxton *(plate 84)*. The Lakelands of Cumbria *(plates 90 to 97)* still hold the souls of their poets, and the great Yorkshire Dales remain unspoilt, shading with solitude the *'bare ruined choirs'* of shattered Fountains Abbey, Bolton Priory and Rievaulx. The very remoteness of their setting – which nowadays makes them so 'romantically sited' – is also their tragedy, for when the monasteries were disbanded in the 16th century there were no parishioners of any nearby town to save the buildings. All honour therefore, to the citizens of Beverley *(plate 88)* and Selby *(plate 89)* who, more than four hundred years ago, had the courage and good sense to buy their monastic churches from the Crown for parochial use. Selby Abbey is built in white magnesian limestone – as encountered at York Minster *(plate 87)* – and today shines like a beacon in the centre of what is otherwise an undistinguished town built almost entirely of brick.

In Northumbria the Pennines merge imperceptibly with the Cheviot Hills, whose remote summits command inspiring views of the River Tweed gliding away to Berwick and the far sea. These hills, which once resounded to the clash of sword and claymore in the fierce hand-to-hand fighting of the Border Wars, now echo only to the cry of the curlew. In summer they 'shade fair' with eglantine and hairbell, and the prevailing colour of the land is stained with the purple of heather and the yellow of vast swags of gorse and broom. Yet in winter's grip – if the moors have not become interfolded acres of drifting snow and hazy blue shadow – the colour of the land takes on a sinister hue, reflecting the predominant granite rocks in bleak greyness, or in the browns of dead bracken. Amid such scenery – where star saxifrage and spring gentians are still to be found – the bold domes of the Cheviots ride across the Scottish border like massive waves. These lands are confusingly called the Lowlands – a description which might suggest flatness and a certain lack of variety, yet nothing could be further from the truth. The Scottish Lowlands – a tableland of grassy hills and cool green pasture that gives shelter to ruined Dryburgh Abbey *(plate 100)*, Culzean Castle *(plate 113)*, and Sir Walter Scott's home at Abbotsford *(plate 101)* – stand in dignity, possessing a loveliness that is apt to be overlooked in comparison with the more dramatic splendours that the rugged northwestern Highlands provide. Yet these Lowlands are more hilly than most parts of England, and the climate, particularly in the central area, can be as harsh in mid-winter – when the first flurries of snow come scudding over the summits of the Tweedsmuir, Lammermuir and Pentland Hills – as that endured by any lonely hamlet in the Highland mountains. Along the line of cliffs at the shore are found fine, old fishing villages which are backed by agricultural land where the traditional white walls of the Scottish farmsteads make a delicious splash against the monotone of pasture and land under plough.

Coming up country from the border, through a land of grey stone and rounded hills, dotted with romantic ruins of long ago – bare skeletons of broken priories and slighted castles – may be seen the jagged frieze of the Highlands (the last stage in the progression through the 'Landscape Below') which rise above the northern horizon; blue and dramatic and unmistakable. Here are found Schiehallion, the Trossachs, the Monadhliaths, Glen Shee *(plate 116)*, the Cairngorms and the isolated mountains of the far north, whose capacity – perhaps an effect of atmospherics – to take on at a distance a wistful, cerulean blue, characterizes all the great mountains of the Heights. These awesome ranges share the landscape with wild kyles and sea lochs that endlessly stud the region and gouge deeply into the land; with icy streams that tumble through green and wooded glens; with frowning crags and darkly shadowed passes; with the calm waters of vast inland lochs – such as Loch Tay *(plate 117)* – and the western seaboard's myriad islands; of Gigha *(plate 118)* and of Columba's sacred Iona *(plate 108)*. Yet above all, it is the ever-changing sky that characterises Highland Scotland and gives rise to an immense variety of shade and subtle hue.

The Severn Estuary in the luminous glow of sunrise **(plate 1)** imparts an urgent sense of the mystery which this commanding seascape demands. It is a place of rushing tides and dangerous currents; and it is not surprising that the Celtic god of the estuary, **Noadu,** survived the Roman occupation, worshipped under the new title **Nodeus.** On Romano-British ornaments she is represented mounted on a seahorse, riding majestically on the crest of the Severn bore.

The medieval richness of **Canterbury (plate 3)** is summarised in the soaring stateliness of the cathedral, whose architecture, from Norman to Perpendicular, is magnificent, and whose 13th-century stained glass is the equal of Bourges and Chartres. On a lesser scale, but with no less pride and piety, the golden sandstone church of **Cranbrook (plate 4)** was raised during the zenith of the cloth-trade, towards the end of the 15th century. As with Henry Dobell's smock windmill of 1814, the medieval church of St Dunstan's still expresses the prosperity of long-dead industries; and the unmistakable air which the Wealden town acquired through commercial success.
Another Wealden village, that of **Penshurst (plate 5)** possesses a Renaissance palace, glorified by the enduring legend of the Elizabethan courtier Sir Philip Sidney, where a half-remembered story of heroic self-denial draws thousands of 'pilgrims' to Penshurst Place each year. The Tudor palace does not dominate the village as it might, but sits discreetly behind the main street, to be seen on entering or leaving the village, yet never obtruding on the scene of modest old houses, an inn and well-proportioned church.

Ramsgate (plate 2) was a fishing village which grew into a Regency resort. In the last century it was greatly enlarged and architecturally there are good things for the admirer of Victoriana, including a church designed by, and the burial place of, Augustus Pugin.

(Overleaf: plates 4 and 5)

Perhaps the finest of all Kent's great houses is at **Knole (plate 6)** in Sevenoaks, where massed vaults of masonry resemble a small town rather than a house. It was originally an archbishop's palace, but it passed to the Sackville family through the gift of Queen Elizabeth I. **Hever Castle (plate 7)**, some ten miles distant from Knole, is also associated with the Virgin Queen, for it was here that her father, Henry VIII, patiently courted and eventually won the hand of her ill-fated mother, Anne. The Tudor brick of **Sissinghurst Castle (plate 9)** has mellowed to a rich, purplish red, and its confused tangle of buildings, with an unusually tall gatehouse, forms a fine backdrop for the gardens created by Victoria Sackville-West. It was she, and her husband Sir Harold Nicolson, who restored the once great manor house and established it as one of the finest gardens in the country – much of it laid out in Elizabethan style. Of especial interest is the white garden, planted entirely with silver-leaved white flowering species, separated by box hedges. At **Scotney Castle (plate 8)** also, there is to be found the happy combination of a landscape of great natural beauty, historic interest, and the rarest harmony of buildings, trees and flowers. The new house, built by Antony Salvin in 1837, has terraces of rhododendrons and azaleas which fall sharply away to the almost unbearably picturesque vista of medieval castle ruins rising from the crystal waters of a lily-covered lake.

(Overleaf: plates 8 and 9)

Of all England's counties Sussex is the easiest to visualise. It lies more or less in four parallel strips, the northern boundary being forest, the next strip the clay weald, then comes the smooth, green line of the Downs – whose rolling, whale-back quality is exemplified at **Storrington (plate 11)** where it recalls Kipling's sentiments: '**bare slopes where chasing shadows skim,/And through the gaps revealed/Belt upon belt, the wooded, dim,/Blue goodness of the weald'**. The final zone comprises the coastline of chalk cliff and low-lying plain.

The streams that flow from the South Downs, though small, have historic import. **Rye (plate 10)**, one of the old Cinque Ports of Sussex, at one time stood at the mouth of its stream, but now, owing to the receding sea, finds itself inland. Here in medieval times the waves lapped at the very foot of the Ypres Tower, yet now the tide breaks some two miles to the south.

At **Bodiam (plate 13)**, a special licence from the Crown enabled Sir Edward Dalyngrigge to build, in 1385, one of the last of the genuine medieval castles, to protect his estate from the incursions of the French. The moat, which is fed by a tributary stream of the River Rother, is still well filled, and together with the gatehouse, walls and drum-towers at the angles, forms one of the most beautiful and evocative castle ruins in Britain.

Plate 12: Leeds Castle in neighbouring Kent.

(Overleaf: plates 12 and 13)

14

A light scattering of snow serves to highlight the formal elegance of **Polesden Lacey (plate 14)**, set in a Surrey landscape once described as **'though deep, yet clear; though gentle, yet not dull; strong without rage; without o'erflowing, full'**. In such terrain, amid Surrey's timbered cottages and Victorian villas with their well-tended gardens, are scattered the county's handful of old and precious towns – Guildford, Dorking, Farnham, Bletchingley and **Reigate (plate 15)**. The latter, although not mentioned by name until the 12th century, was a manor of the powerful de Warenne family, Earls of Surrey in the reign of William the Conqueror. Here they built a strongly fortified castle where, according to legend, the barons deliberated before their encounter with King John at Runnymede and the signing of the **Magna Carta**. Sadly nothing now remains of Reigate's castle, save for the mound on which it once stood, whose dry fosse and traces of moat are well picked out by the effects of snow, low winter shadow and the aerial perspective.

19

On the north bank of the grey ribbon of the Thames, which threads its course past sprawling Victorian wharves, stands London's medieval heart, which now constitutes that richest part of the capital known simply as **'The City' (plates 16 and 19).** The mercantile square mile has at its centre Wren's Classical masterpiece, **St Paul's Cathedral (plate 18),** which rose like a phoenix from the ashes of the Great Fire of London to dominate the Stuart capital.

Today's 'temples of mammon', in the form of unfortunate and ill-conceived glass towers, poke their intrusive heads above the City's stone and concrete jungle, yet for all their height they fail to overshadow Wren's glorious dome.

On the City's eastern boundary stands the dizzy prospect of **'Her Majesty's Tower of London' (plate 17)** – a grey, uneven maze, harsh in the texture of its stone, rugged with crenellations and dark with sinister association.

(Previous pages: plates 16 and 17)

The enormous, twin glass roofs of **Victoria Railway Station (plate 20, centre)** span a concourse teeming with commuters from the southern Home Counties and from Brighton (which is but an hour's journey away). Within five minutes walk of the rush-hour **maelstrom** may be found peaceful haunts of solitude in the silence of St James's Park and Green Park whose tree-filled acres spread to surround the honeyed stone of Buckingham Palace, the residence of sovereigns since the reign of George II, and once described by Pepys as **'a country house in summer, and a town house in winter'**.

From the leafy seclusion of St James's, southeast across Whitehall, the eye scans the architecture of England at the height of Empire until it is arrested by the enormous neo-Gothic form of the **Palace of Westminster (plate 21)**, standing cheek by jowl with Westminster Hall. The latter was originally raised by William Rufus and altered by Richard II, who feasted ten thousand of London's poor there daily during the Christmastide of 1398. Westminster Hall has since been the scene of some of the most famous trials in England's history.

Opposite the Red King's Hall is Westminster Abbey, London's one entirely beautiful possession. Built originally by the saintly Edward the Confessor, it was massively and elaborately enlarged by Henry III. This **'short, stout and ungainly old man with a blinking left eye'** has here left to us, by his munificence and foresight, a promise of permanence in a world of change.

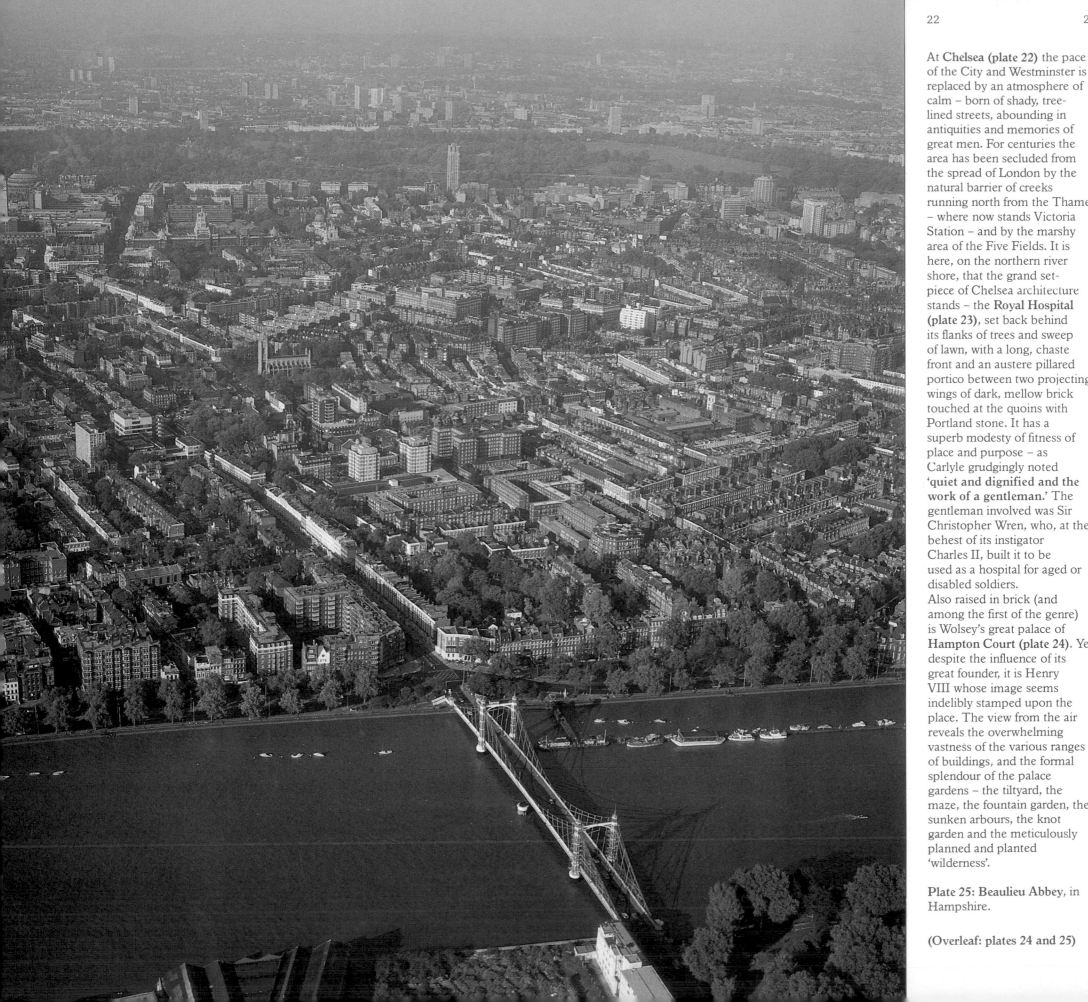

At **Chelsea (plate 22)** the pace of the City and Westminster is replaced by an atmosphere of calm – born of shady, tree-lined streets, abounding in antiquities and memories of great men. For centuries the area has been secluded from the spread of London by the natural barrier of creeks running north from the Thames – where now stands Victoria Station – and by the marshy area of the Five Fields. It is here, on the northern river shore, that the grand set-piece of Chelsea architecture stands – the **Royal Hospital (plate 23)**, set back behind its flanks of trees and sweep of lawn, with a long, chaste front and an austere pillared portico between two projecting wings of dark, mellow brick touched at the quoins with Portland stone. It has a superb modesty of fitness of place and purpose – as Carlyle grudgingly noted **'quiet and dignified and the work of a gentleman.'** The gentleman involved was Sir Christopher Wren, who, at the behest of its instigator Charles II, built it to be used as a hospital for aged or disabled soldiers.

Also raised in brick (and among the first of the genre) is Wolsey's great palace of **Hampton Court (plate 24)**. Yet, despite the influence of its great founder, it is Henry VIII whose image seems indelibly stamped upon the place. The view from the air reveals the overwhelming vastness of the various ranges of buildings, and the formal splendour of the palace gardens – the tiltyard, the maze, the fountain garden, the sunken arbours, the knot garden and the meticulously planned and planted 'wilderness'.

Plate 25: Beaulieu Abbey, in Hampshire.

(Overleaf: plates 24 and 25)

27

The New Forest, created by William the Conqueror in 1079 as an enormous hunting park, covers the whole of the beheaded triangle of Hampshire enclosed by the rivers Blackwater and Avon, the Channel and Southampton Water. It is not, as one might suppose, an unbroken tract of woodland, but the area's fascination is in its richness of variety. Here we have open parkland, stretches of bracken, heather hummocks glowing pink in summer, and noble avenues of stately trees. Clustered within this land of variation – where wild ponies graze and roam at will through oak-fringed glades where kings once hunted – are the woodland-lapped villages of **Brockenhurst (plate 27)** and **Lyndhurst (plate 26)** the capital of the New Forest. The former has a fine church of Norman origin which claims to be the oldest foundation in the forest. Brockenhurst is principally renowned, however, for the grave of Brusher Mills, the famous New Forest snake-catcher responsible for the demise of over three thousand adders. **(Overleaf: plates 28 and 29)**

31

Oxfordshire is the county for the lover of noble architecture. Its churches stand out as the finest among the shires. Its manor houses, too, represent every style of architecture, from Vanburgh's monumental **Blenheim Palace (plate 32)** to the gentle Elizabethan brick of **Mapledurham House (plate 33)**; the inspiration for Grahame's 'Toad Hall'.

Henley (plate 31) is also set in the beautiful wooded countryside of the Thames Valley, yet it is to the **City of Oxford (plates 28 and 29)** that the eye turns for the supreme delights of architecture. Here, among a forest of **'dreaming spires and pinnacles'**, is breathtaking beauty – in the unsurpassed, broad sweep of the 'High', past Magdalen

College and Queen's College on the one hand, and University College on the other. From Carfax, where four roads meet, it is but a stone's throw to Tom Tower; the entrance to Christ Church with its Cathedral, and the big quad at Balliol.
Plate 30: Chipping Campden.
(Overleaf: plates 32 and 33)

Upon the bare scarp of the Wiltshire Plain a low sun and harsh shadows dramatise the huge megaliths of **Stonehenge (plate 37)**. An aerial view wonderfully reveals the encircling ditch and bank that date from the Stone Age – upon which the stupendous Bronze Age temple was later developed into circles of sarsen stones around a horseshoe of trilithons enclosing the enigmatic Welsh bluestones. To the south, in the Valley of Avon, the cathedral city of **Salisbury (plate 34)** is almost encircled by the vastness of the downs, so that from whatever direction it is approached, the tall, captivating spire (at 404ft the tallest of any cathedral in Britain) provides the first intimation of the city. Indeed, Salisbury has no history earlier than its cathedral, for both were planned upon a virgin site in the water-meads of the Avon, when the hilltop town of Old Sarum was abandoned during the 13th century.

One of the most magnificent tombs within the cathedral is that of Sir Thomas Gorges and his wife, Helena. It is they who, in 1573, commenced the building of the romantic castle at **Longford (plate 36)** a few miles downstream from Salisbury. The peculiar design is based upon the shield of the Holy Trinity, and the cost of its construction almost ruined Sir Thomas. However, when a Spanish galleon was wrecked while he was Governor of Hurst Castle, his wife begged the hull from Queen Elizabeth. The ship was later discovered to be full of silver bars, and with this fortune Longford Castle was completed in 1591.

Plate 35: the elegant market town of **Marlborough**.

(Overleaf: plates 36 and 37)

At **Wilton House (plate 38)** and, more especially, at **Stourhead (plate 39)** – both in Wiltshire – the English landscape gardens of the early 18th century were invented. Their abiding spirit is the most poetic of all the dreams of antiquity, the most transporting evocation in the living form of nature of Claude and Poussin's two-dimensional art.

The great picture garden was begun at Wilton by the 9th Earl of Pembroke, whose elegant Palladian bridge spans the River Nadder; and at Stourhead by Henry Hoare in 1740. Stourhead is the first of the completely informal landscape compositions which were the special English contribution to the art of gardening. At the centre of Stourhead's three-armed lake, the Doric Temple of Flora reflects its Tuscan portico in the smooth waters at its feet, and nearby can be seen the Pantheon, shining against its luxuriant, wooded background. High above the surface of the lake, amid dense trees, is seen the circular Temple of the Sun, after the original at Baalbek.

St Ives (plate 40) has been a magnet for artists since the 1880s, when painters were lured here by the delights of its crisp, clear light. The best part of the town is on the neck of land between the harbour and the surfing beach of Porthmeor. The streets are narrow, and on either side of the steep alleys are galleries founded by the artist community.

From Trencrom Hill three miles to the south, there are splendid views over the Hayle Estuary; west to the high haunts of prehistoric man and tinners, and south to St Michael's Mount (plate 42). This lofty, isolated mass of rock, some twenty-one acres in extent, is crowned by the most romantically sited of all medieval castles. At high water St Michael's Mount is separated from the mainland by a 500ft stretch of water, but at low tide a cobblestone causeway connects the two: this may be seen in the photograph as a very fine line running beneath the sea's surface. The mount has ever been a place of romance and mystery, having associatons with Christ's legendary journey to Glastonbury. It lies at the terminus of a 'primary ley', aligned to the Mayday sunrise, which intersects, (without deviating from its course) the prehistoric monuments of Brent Tor, Cadbury Hill, Glastonbury and Avebury, as well as passing through the chancels of many churches dedicated to the dragon-killing St Michael and St George.

Plate 43: Coverack is a typical fishing village complete with stone-built, whitewashed cottages, a miniature harbour and a lifeboat station.

Plate 41: Pendeen Watch.

(Overleaf: plates 42 and 43)

45

By reason of their inaccessibility the Cornish coves of **Talland Bay (plate 44)** and **Cadgwith (plate 47)** are among the least known places in the Duchy. The former has been the scene of many wrecks, and the latter is reached down a narrow, winding lane which opens suddenly to the miniature cove. Cadgwith lies at the mouth of a well-wooded valley and its compact little village of thatched, stone-built cottages – unspoilt by the march of time – is tucked neatly between high, rugged cliffs. Two small beaches are separated by 'The Todden', a diminutive headland leading to a secluded natural bathing pool hidden among the rocks.

The summer sun reflects on the wind-blown ripples of the Helford River at **Porth Navas (plate 46)** and upon the wide ocean at the **Longships Lighthouse (plate 45)**. However, such tranquillity belies the true nature of the seas around the Cornish coast, and in severe storms waves have been known to lash the 110ft-high lantern of the Longships' light. **(Overleaf: plates 46 and 47)**

49

No ancient town of England has preserved its medieval atmosphere to the same degree as **Wells (plate 48)** in Somerset. It takes as its centrepiece the soaring cathedral whose renowned West Front is the most ornate of any in the realm, and upon which is displayed the most extensive array of medieval sculpture to have survived the Reformation.

Wells possesses a fine example of a medieval close, surrounded by the houses of cathedral dignitaries. To the north lie the drum-like Chapter House and a row of lodgings built for the vicar's choral; to the south stand the cloisters and the partly rebuilt Bishop's Palace surrounded by its moat.

As if to mirror the spirit of Wells' Great West Front, the Elizabethan Manor House at **Montacute (plate 49)** exhibits carved statues of the Nine Worthies – Joshua, David, Judas Maccabeus, Hector, Alexander, Julius Caesar, Arthur, Charlemagne and Godfrey de Bouillon – within Ham stone niches on its eastern face.

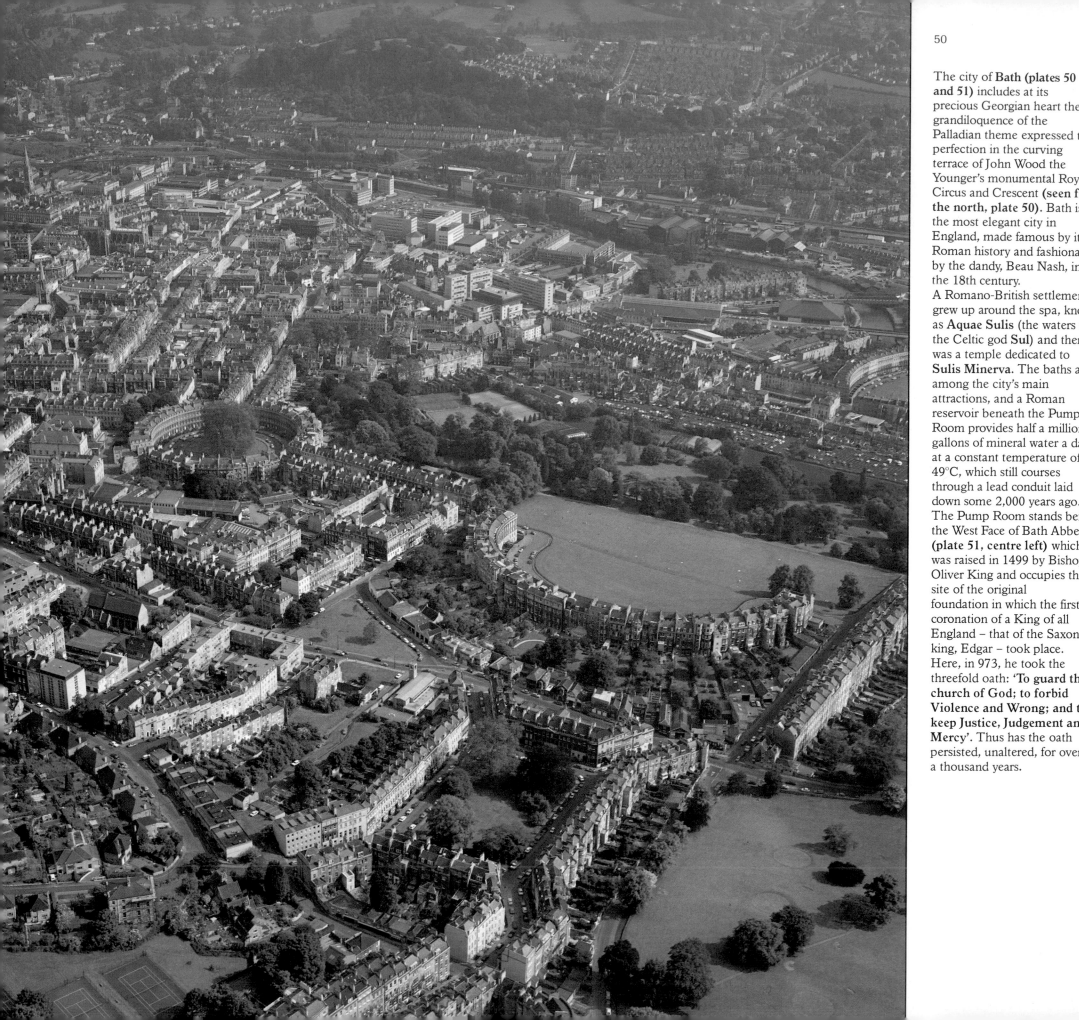

The city of **Bath (plates 50 and 51)** includes at its precious Georgian heart the grandiloquence of the Palladian theme expressed to perfection in the curving terrace of John Wood the Younger's monumental Royal Circus and Crescent **(seen from the north, plate 50)**. Bath is the most elegant city in England, made famous by its Roman history and fashionable by the dandy, Beau Nash, in the 18th century.

A Romano-British settlement grew up around the spa, known as **Aquae Sulis** (the waters of the Celtic god **Sul**) and there was a temple dedicated to **Sulis Minerva**. The baths are among the city's main attractions, and a Roman reservoir beneath the Pump Room provides half a million gallons of mineral water a day at a constant temperature of 49°C, which still courses through a lead conduit laid down some 2,000 years ago. The Pump Room stands before the West Face of Bath Abbey **(plate 51, centre left)** which was raised in 1499 by Bishop Oliver King and occupies the site of the original foundation in which the first coronation of a King of all England – that of the Saxon king, Edgar – took place. Here, in 973, he took the threefold oath: **'To guard the church of God; to forbid Violence and Wrong; and to keep Justice, Judgement and Mercy'.** Thus has the oath persisted, unaltered, for over a thousand years.

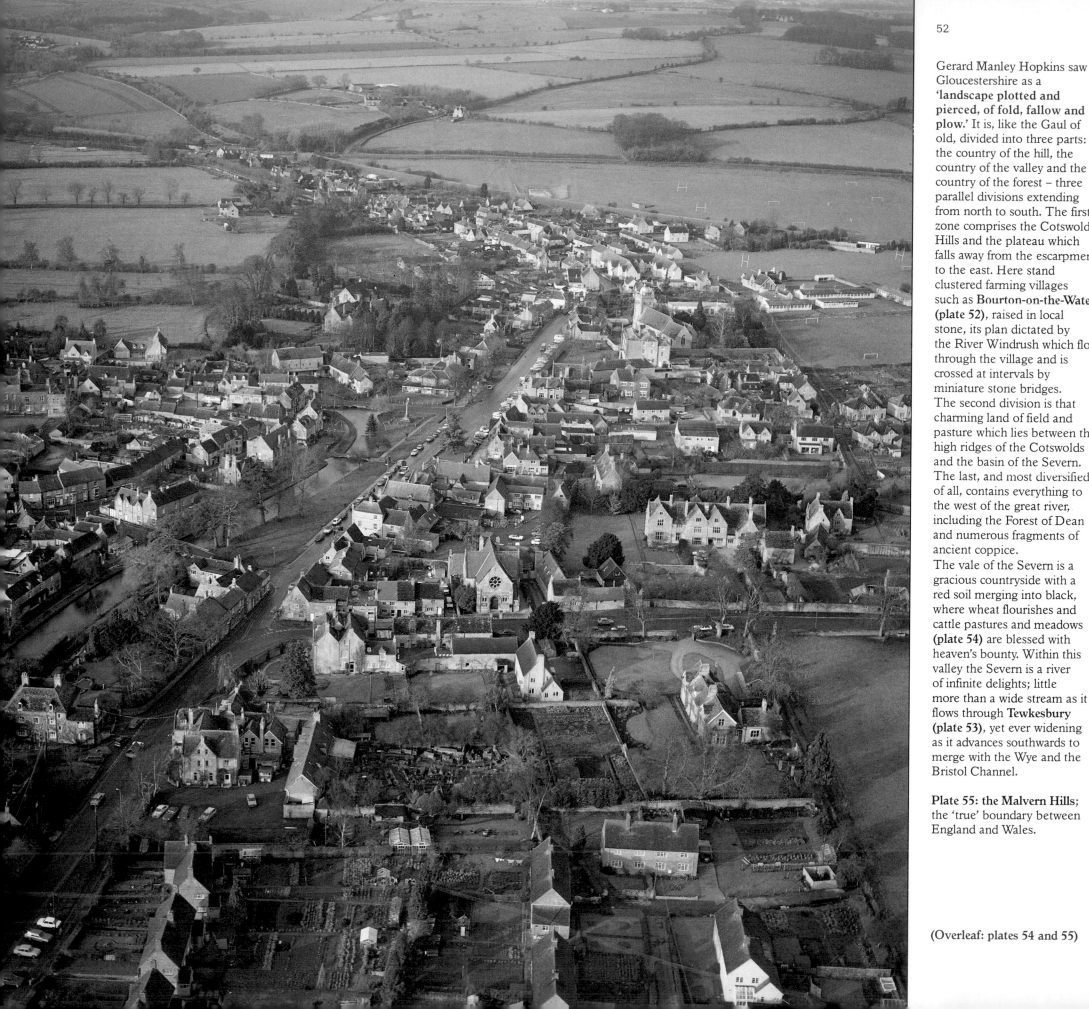

Gerard Manley Hopkins saw Gloucestershire as a 'landscape plotted and pierced, of fold, fallow and plow.' It is, like the Gaul of old, divided into three parts: the country of the hill, the country of the valley and the country of the forest – three parallel divisions extending from north to south. The first zone comprises the Cotswold Hills and the plateau which falls away from the escarpment to the east. Here stand clustered farming villages such as **Bourton-on-the-Water (plate 52)**, raised in local stone, its plan dictated by the River Windrush which flows through the village and is crossed at intervals by miniature stone bridges.

The second division is that charming land of field and pasture which lies between the high ridges of the Cotswolds and the basin of the Severn. The last, and most diversified of all, contains everything to the west of the great river, including the Forest of Dean and numerous fragments of ancient coppice.

The vale of the Severn is a gracious countryside with a red soil merging into black, where wheat flourishes and cattle pastures and meadows **(plate 54)** are blessed with heaven's bounty. Within this valley the Severn is a river of infinite delights; little more than a wide stream as it flows through **Tewkesbury (plate 53)**, yet ever widening as it advances southwards to merge with the Wye and the Bristol Channel.

Plate 55: the Malvern Hills; the 'true' boundary between England and Wales.

(Overleaf: plates 54 and 55)

With the exception of London, Warwickshire probably receives more visitors than any other county in England. This is due not only to its scenic attractions but also to its historical associations. A mere list of names – Warwick, Kenilworth, Coventry, Rugby and Stratford-upon-Avon – conjure up visions from the past. Understandably, the greatest of these concerns Shakespeare, and the Bard's association with his native **Stratford-upon-Avon (plate 58)** has turned the sleepy dormitory town into a centre of 20th-century pilgrimage. There are ghosts to be summoned at Rugby too – both factual and fictional – which dwell in the great, rambling pile of **Rugby School (plate 56)**. The architecture of four centuries is reflected in its varied walls, and it is neither difficult to hark back in one's imagination to the time of Dr Arnold and **Tom Brown's Schooldays**, nor hard to visualize the emergence of Rugby Football as a game when, in 1823, a young schoolboy, William Webb Ellis, '**with a fine disregard of the rules of football as played in his time first took the ball in his arms and ran with it.**'

Plate 57: Birmingham city centre.

Plate 59: Warwick Castle, the gaunt stronghold of the Beauchamp Earls of Warwick; reputed to be one of the finest medieval fortresses in Europe.

(Overleaf: plates 58 and 59)

61

Just as the south coast of Wales has its castles stretching from the Marches to the ocean boundary, so has North Wales a string of concentric Plantagenet fortresses – at Conway, Beaumaris, Rhuddlan, Caernarvon and Harlech – but these are of a quite different order. The former were as much baronial mansions as fortresses, whilst the latter, built by Edward I

after his conquest of the Principality of North Wales, were massively-fortified bastions for the protection of royal troops against hostile, native Celts. Indeed, at **Conway (plate 60)** it was not only the castle that was protected from Welsh revolt, but also the medieval town.

At **Rhuddlan Castle (plate 61)** Edward I organised his

administration of Wales, secure behind its massive twin gatehouses and curtain walls enclosed by a moat. However, of all the King's military constructions, it is **Harlech Castle (plate 62)** that has the most impressive setting.
Plate 63: Pembroke, the town and castle.
(Overleaf: plates 62 and 63)

Under the yoke of Plantagenet kings the flower of Celtic independence retreated into the fastness of the Snowdonia landscape, with its vast mountains, notched in places like battlemented towers, high passes and craggy peaks – like the summit of **Tryfan (plate 65)** – whence the spirit of Welsh freedom occasionally resurfaced in the guise of her hero princes: Llyweln the Great, Llywelyn ap Gruffydd and Owain Glyndwr. Some part of this essence of defiance seems to linger in these wild northern mountains, where deep, rock-girt cwms are bejewelled with gleaming tarns, such as Llyn Llydaw in **The Snowdon Horseshoe (plate 64)**. There is an all-pervading silence here, save for the bleat of lambs, the sudden flight of snipe, or the solitary call of the rare red kite – described by one native as **'the living flame of the sky'**. Soaring above all – dominating all – is the ethereal mass of Snowdon, the focus of bardic song and sentiment throughout the ages.

There is majesty, also, at the sea's edge – where the cold, green swell of the Atlantic ceaselessly breaks against the tiny islet of **South Stack (plate 67)** – with its lighthouse of 1809 – and in the sapphire seas to the west of **Solva (plate 66)**, whose unpredictable moods have lured many ships to grief on its shores.

(Previous pages: plates 64 and 65)

Well demonstrating the
influence that man can have
upon the face of the landscape
are the oil terminals at
Milford Haven (plate 68),
which are the largest of their
kind in Britain, and Sir
Clough William-Ellis'
Mediterranean fantasy of
Portmeirion (plate 69). The
one dominates the scene and
oppresses the sensibilities,
whilst the other seems to
exalt the spirit.

Angelsey is connected to the
mainland by two famous
bridges: Robert Stephenson's
Britannia Bridge carrying the
railway, and Thomas Telford's
**Menai Suspension Bridge (plate
71)**, which has carried the
road from London to Holyhead
since 1826. Telford's bridge
is his most famous and
influential work, and is of
cast iron supported by sixteen
wrought-iron chains passing
over tall masonry towers on
either bank and anchored below
ground. A similarly courageous
engineering feat led to the
construction of **Holyhead
Harbour (plate 70)** whose
Refuge – a one-and-a-half-
mile-long, solid masonry
breakwater – is the result of
twenty-eight years incessant
labour. The port is, today, a
major terminal for ferries to
Ireland.

(Overleaf: plates 70 and 71)

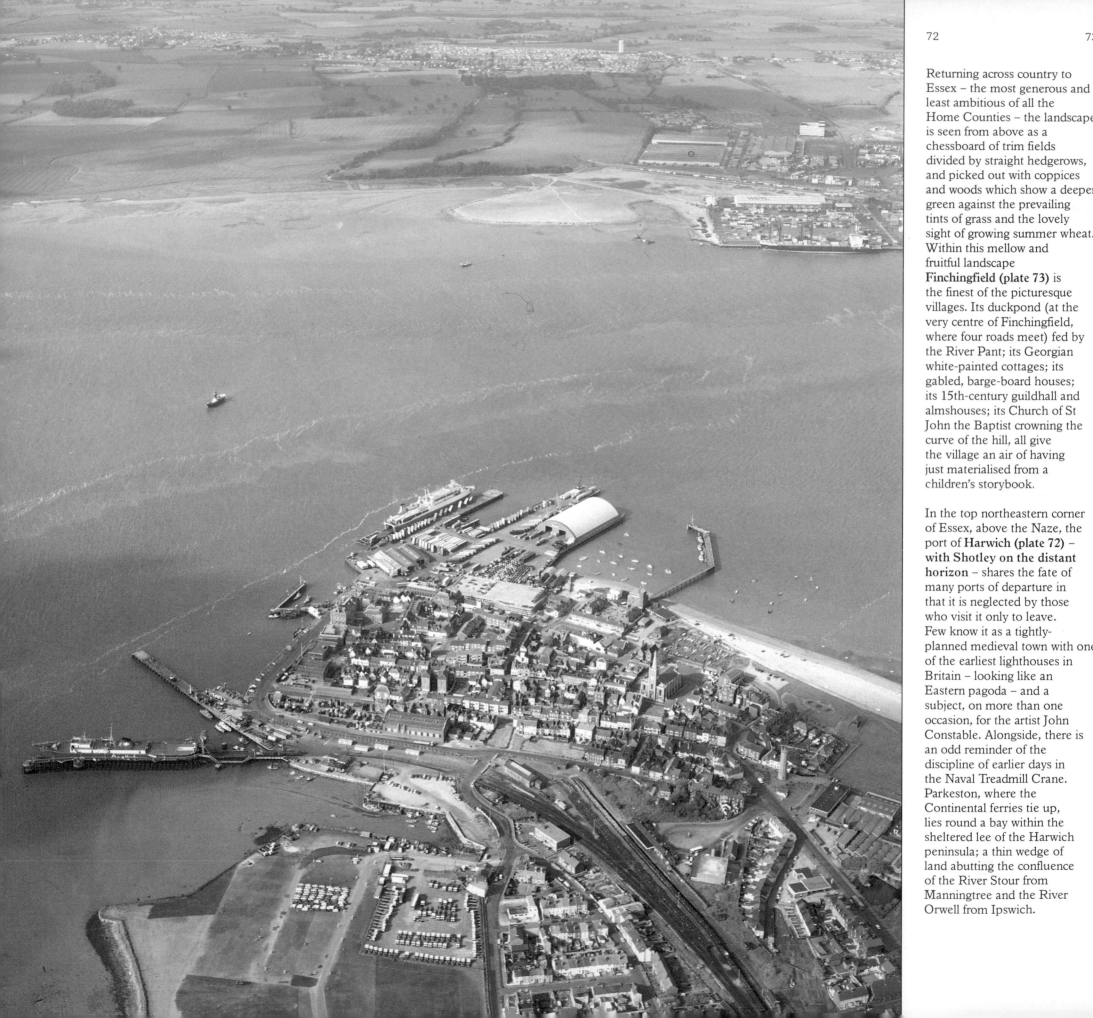

Returning across country to
Essex – the most generous and
least ambitious of all the
Home Counties – the landscape
is seen from above as a
chessboard of trim fields
divided by straight hedgerows,
and picked out with coppices
and woods which show a deeper
green against the prevailing
tints of grass and the lovely
sight of growing summer wheat.
Within this mellow and
fruitful landscape
Finchingfield (plate 73) is
the finest of the picturesque
villages. Its duckpond (at the
very centre of Finchingfield,
where four roads meet) fed by
the River Pant; its Georgian
white-painted cottages; its
gabled, barge-board houses;
its 15th-century guildhall and
almshouses; its Church of St
John the Baptist crowning the
curve of the hill, all give
the village an air of having
just materialised from a
children's storybook.

In the top northeastern corner
of Essex, above the Naze, the
port of **Harwich (plate 72) –
with Shotley on the distant
horizon** – shares the fate of
many ports of departure in
that it is neglected by those
who visit it only to leave.
Few know it as a tightly-
planned medieval town with one
of the earliest lighthouses in
Britain – looking like an
Eastern pagoda – and a
subject, on more than one
occasion, for the artist John
Constable. Alongside, there is
an odd reminder of the
discipline of earlier days in
the Naval Treadmill Crane.
Parkeston, where the
Continental ferries tie up,
lies round a bay within the
sheltered lee of the Harwich
peninsula; a thin wedge of
land abutting the confluence
of the River Stour from
Manningtree and the River
Orwell from Ipswich.

The best way to view **Norwich (plate 74)** is to look down upon it, either from the air, or as George Borrow loved to look down, from the heights of Mousehold Heath. It is still a rural capital; a medieval town which is really an amalgam of villages clinging to their old country names – St Miles Coslany, St John's Timberhill, St Clement's-at-the-Fye-Bridge, St James-in-Pockthorpe – each clustered about its parish church (of which Norwich has more than any other city north of the Alps), and at the parochial centre rises the marvellous cathedral set amid the calm, though somewhat commercial, oasis of the Close.

To travel northwestwards from the Norfolk capital is to traverse a landscape of settled fields draining into dykes, rivers and immense, unhampered skylines. Here are found the splendours of Houghton and **Holkham Hall (plate 77)** set in their great parks. Here and there lie smaller, well-wooded estates, and every mile or so brick and flint cottages clustered into a village, or set in groups around some great medieval ruin, as at Castle Rising.

The earthworks at **Castle Rising (plate 76)**, upon which the Norman motte and bailey castle was superimposed, are some of the most spectacular in England and their scale can only fully be appreciated from the air. The site has yet to be excavated in full and, although the smaller enclosures to the east and west suggest a Roman influence, the origins of the main earthworks remain uncertain.

Plate 75: Norfolk's most influential port of the Middle Ages, **King's Lynn.**

(Overleaf: plates 76 and 77)

In Cambridge and Ely the county of Cambridgeshire has two of the most historic cities in Britain. Each is master of the landscape it commands. In the north of the shire **Ely (plate 78)** has a cathedral whose soaring western tower and octagon are visible for miles around, its stonework and white roof shining out against the dark, alluvial soil of the Fens, across wide fields of sweet grazing and root crops, where dykes cut as straight as the flight of an arrow.

In the south of the county **Cambridge (plates 80 and 81)** is held within a softening landscape of rolling chalk hills watered by tiny streams. The town is often compared to Oxford, yet the two have few similarities and depend for their beauty on quite different circumstances. Oxford is a great city in which the university buildings stand out from the banality of much of the town. Cambridge, on the other hand, is a small city in which the university buildings and churches seem to form the greater part. Among its treasures are the ancient brickwork of Magdalene College (a reminder of the former Benedictine hostel); the varied architecture and quadrangles of Trinity College; the old court of Corpus Christi; the modern chapel of Pembroke College, built to the design of Sir Christopher Wren; the 17th-century chapel of Peterhouse and, supreme above all others, the Perpendicular chapel of **King's College Cambridge (plate 80, centre)** with its fan-vaulted ceiling, and elegant lawns running down to the willow-shrouded banks of the Cam.

Plate 79: the Fen landscape near Boston.

(Overleaf: plates 80 and 81)

No one looking at the view of **Lincoln (plate 83)** can fail to be struck by the dominant position of the cathedral on its high ridge above the town and encircling fenlands of the Witham Valley. Here, in a materialistic and fragmented age, it testifies to the unifying spiritual belief in the Lord which, at the time of its construction, gave meaning and proportion to every aspect of life. The exquisitely pale colour – almost a shimmering silver haze – of the beautiful Ancaster and Lincoln limestone in which the cathedral is raised is a splendid foil to the pantiles of the secular buildings which huddle around its massive bulk; reminders of the trading connections between England and Flanders which first brought pantile roofing to the eastern districts during the 17th century.

The open space below the cathedral, known as Minster Yard, is full of interest. It was the site, in the Roman town of **Lindum Colonia**, of the great colonnade. Abutting the cathedral's Great West Front – whose tremendous breadth and elaboration is similar to the facades of Italian Renaissance churches – is the 14th-century Exchequer Gate, the largest of the gates in the encircling city wall, built soon after 1285 when the cathedral was granted a licence to fortify its precincts. Within this enclosure are still to be seen a fine tithe barn of c1440 and the ancient, Bishop's Palace.

Plate 82: Boston – Lincolnshire's ancient port, raised to medieval prominence by the lucrative wool trade with the Low Countries.

84

85

Positioned within the lovely moorland countryside of the
Peaks, the spa town of **Buxton (plate 84)** is the highest in
the kingdom. It is sheltered by hills even higher than its
1,007ft site, yet is able to offer gentle scenery more
typical of the lowlands alongside sedate reaches of the
lovely River Wye. **Ladybower Reservoir (plate 85)** is one such
spot; where the russet of the bracken-covered limestone
peaks is relieved by milder shades of green in the vale
below.
The town itself is built around the thermal and chalybeate
spring whose medicinal properties were exploited to the
benefit of the town towards the end of the 18th century,
when Buxton rivalled the elegant supremacy of Bath. The pale
blue waters bubble up from a mile underground at the rate of
a quarter of a million gallons a day. The town's
architectural development was largely at the instigation of
the 5th Duke of Devonshire, who built the beautiful
Crescent, the Pump Rooms and the Devonshire Royal Hospital.

Within the borders of Yorkshire, now three counties, is a wealth of outstanding and diversified beauty; of bleak gritstone fells thrown into contrast against long, lovely dales; of colliery towns – that feed the power stations of Drax, Eggborough and **Ferrybridge (plate 86)** – contrasting with the medieval heritage of **York (plate 87)**, Beverley and

Selby. The former has at its heart that **'jewel of light and glass'**, the High Minster of York; whilst **Selby (plate 89)** in North Yorkshire has a Benedictine Abbey of no less renown. The Minster at **Beverley (plate 88)** is still very much the focal point of the East Riding (although now officially incorporated in Humberside) and is one of the finest Gothic

churches in Europe. Less than a mile to the northwest, along Beverley's main street, is the Church of St Mary **(plate 88, centre, top)** which challenges St Mary Redcliffe and Boston for the accolade of finest parish church in England.

(Overleaf: plates 88 and 89)

Lakeland, filled with the souls of her poets, is a landscape where atmosphere paints its own unique images upon the scene. The glass-like reflections of the lakes themselves are the most enigmatic, where 'Nought wakens or disturbs their tranquil tides, Nought but the char that for the may-fly leaps and breaks the mirror of the circling deep'. The

surfaces of lakes such as **Rydal Water (plate 93)**, **Derwent Water (plate 90)** and **Ullswater (plate 9l)** possess a piercing turquoise sheen that is not a reflection of the sky, although it may be enhanced by it just as it is changed and patterned by every breath of wind.
One of the most spectacular lakes is **Buttermere (plate 92)**

which lies like a stretched silken cloth below Great Gable. Here, with snow on the ancient volcanic rocks, and sculptured, marble-like cliffs gathered on all sides, it comes close to the primeval state of glacial desolation.

(Overleaf: plates 92 and 93)

It is the archaic setting of low, habitable dale, set against the fierce magnitude of mountain scenery which gives the English Lakes their wistful appeal. There is never a season when the land does not offer up treasures – whether in springtime's unfolding of bud along the lake shore, when hazel and birch flush purple; or in summer's richness of green and brilliant array of wild flowers. In June and July old packhorse lanes are radiant with wild rose, foxglove, honeysuckle, campion, comfrey, speedwell and the dainty yellow poppy. At such times **Ullswater (plate 96)** and **Thirlmere (plate 94)** are especially noted for the glory of their shores. Even in the depths of winter the area keeps it charms, and this time of year is arguably the best, for never does the mountain scenery of the east ridge of **Pillar Fell (plates 95 and 97)** with **Wastwater** in the background appear to better advantage than when dusted in snow and the lakes at their feet are transparent with ice. Glints of sunshine invest their surface with colourful change, making them as opal set in virgin white; towards sunset the snow-clad fells assume every tint the sun can create, from deepest crimson to palest gold.

(Overleaf: plates 96 and 97)

Scotland possesses one of the most magical and yet one of the most terrifying landscapes. Her Highlands, as at **Ben Vorlich (plate 99)**, remain snow capped for much of the year; jagged friezes of mountain and moorland which, however imposing, are at certain seasons so hostile that their wilderness depresses rather than exalts the spirit. In the

southern lands a softer, more poetic light informs scenes of a picturesque splendour with a strange and irrepressible charm – such as that which surrounds Sir Walter Scott's country house at **Abbotsford (plate 101)**. Indeed, the whole of the Lowlands seem touched by the spirit of the great author's historical romances, for the countryside appears

everywhere to be dominated by its past and studded with medieval remains – of the bare skeletons of broken abbeys, like that at **Dryburgh (plate 100)**; and towering fortresses such as **Stirling (plate 98)** which looks out from its rocky pinnacle over the greatest field of Scottish valour; Bannockburn. **(Overleaf: plates 100 and 101)**

Edinburgh Castle (plate 102), perched on a great volcanic outcrop of rock, overlooks the Old Town with its parallel thoroughfares of Hanover and Castle Street directing the eye past the Royal Circus to the distant quay of Granton Harbour on the Firth. The citadel so crowns the promontory that it is precipitous on three sides, and so well defended on the fourth that, throughout the centuries of medieval warfare, its summit remained inaccessible to attacking forces – save on two occasions – in 1296 when it fell to King Edward I of England, and forty-five years later, when it was recaptured by the Scots. Thus has the gaunt pile dominated the citizens of Edinburgh with an air at once threatening and protective; ready to assume either role, depending on the sympathies of its garrison.

Plate 103: the view over Edinburgh from Dean Bridge on the Queensferry Road, past the dome of the West Register House to the Salisbury Crags and the summit of Arthur's Seat.

105

The road and rail lines that span the Forth west of Edinburgh are carried across the Firth of Tay at **Dundee (plate 105)** by the graceful, two-mile-long, Victorian Tay Railway Bridge of 1887 and, eighty years its junior, the Tay Road Bridge which brings traffic right into the very heart of 'Scotland's Third City'.

Where the Tay meets the North Sea, the headland of Fife sends golden fringes of sand around the coastline of the Ness; and it is here, on the northern shore, that the Royal Burgh of **St Andrews (plates 106 and 107)** stands. For many people the town spells nothing but golf – for its incomparable links make it the mecca of the followers of the

Royal and Ancient Game. St Andrews, however, is also the spiritual centre of Scotland – even though its cathedral now lies in ruins beside the quay **(plate 107, centre)** – and boasts the oldest university in the country.
Plate 104: the Forth Road and Rail Bridges.
(Overleaf: plates 106 and 107)

The Isles of the Western Coast possess a beauty which is all their own; an effect of light playing upon the sea. Near at hand the water is vivid blue, or even turquoise where the yellow of the shore changes the sea's hue, as seen at Baile Mor on St Columba's **Iona (plate 108)**. As the sea recedes so its very depth changes its colour to a deep violet, or an indigo sheen which serves to intensify the green of low isles like **Bute (plate 110)**, and throws into contrast the white sand bars of **Scaraster Bay (plate 109)** on South Harris.
Rothesay (plate 111) has given its name to the Prince of Wales' dukedom and, sited on sandy Rothesay Bay, it is the principal town of the Isle of Bute. The harbour is full of small craft in July, when the Clyde Yachting Fortnight is in full swing and steamers call at the pier. Nearby is Rothesay Castle which, when seen from above, stands out from the town as a green square with a moated fortress at its centre. There are four round towers linked by a curtain wall enclosing a circular courtyard and keep. The Normans stormed the castle in 1240, only to lose it some twenty-three years later to King Haco of Norway. The building was taken in turn by Robert the Bruce in the early 14th century.

Overleaf: plates 110 and 111)

Of Aberdeen's two rivers, the Dee is more famous than the Don, for it flows through the open-hearted, gracious landscape so beloved and popularized by Queen Victoria. Realizing that her heart was in the Highlands, she resolved to make a home at Balmoral. The Prince Consort purchased the estate in 1852 for £31,000 and had the old house (first mentioned in 1484 and known as **Bouchmorale**, which is appropriately Gaelic for **majestic dwelling**) rebuilt in his own fantasised version of the Scottish Baronial style. The resultant chateau-like mansion of **Balmoral Castle (plate 112)** is rich in 'fairy story' turrets and gables and, lying on a large sweeping curve of the River Dee, is surrounded by pine woods, heather moors and sombre expanses of deer forest.

Plate 113: Culzean Castle, on the Strathclyde coast is a typical product of the 18th-century Picturesque style.

Sited at the confluence of the Rivers Leven and Clyde, **Dumbarton (plate 114)** was once the centre of the independent Kingdom of Strathclyde, and has a royal castle standing on the majestic, 240ft-high Dumbarton Rock **(plate 114, centre)**. To the west is the port of **Tarbert (plate 115)**, the centre of the Loch Fyne herring industry. It lies on the tiny isthmus on the shores of East Loch Tarbert – the little neck of land linking Knapdale with Kintyre. Magnus Barefoot of Norway is said to have been ceremonially dragged by his warriors in a longship from Tarbert across this isthmus in 1093 – a distance of nearly two miles.

(Overleaf: plates 114 and 115)

It does not take the road at **Glen Shee (plate 116)** long to rise out of its vale to the high country of the mountains. As at **Loch Tay (plate 117)** under a cloak of snow, it is not a comfortable scene that meets the eye, but one to marvel at in all its gaunt and threatening majesty.

At **Gigha Island (plate 118)** the view is westwards across the Sound of Jura to distant Islay. **Tobermory (plate 119)** 'The Well of Mary' is the chief town on the Island of Mull. It was founded in 1788 by the Society for the Encouragement of the British Fisheries, but failed to realise the hopes of its founders and has never been an important fishing station. It stands on the shore of a bay in which one of the galleons of the Spanish Armada was blown up and sunk in 1588 by Donald Glas MacLean.

Plate 120: Hadrian's Wall, which runs from Tyne to Solway undeterred by crag or precipice, and admits no interruption. **(Following pages: plates 118, 119 and 120)**